CHOCOLATE CHIPS

Contemporary Haiku

Michael Moore

*To Marsha
Thank you for your
Kindness and your support
Michael Moore
1998*

Mustard Seed
Press

Also by Michael Moore

Your line, Your Move
Chocolate Haiku
Home Grown in The Haiku Garden
Contemporary View of Haiku-
  (Bilingual English & Spanish)

Edited by Windy Barker

Copyright © 1995 by Michael Moore

Published by Mustard Seed Press 1998

ISBN 0-910702-4-2

6   5   4   3   2

For haiku workshop information
write to, P.O. Box 681694,
San Antonio, Tx., 78268-1694

Contents

Introduction

Chocolate Chips is a collection of three hundred poems. It is a contemporary expression of a Japanese art form. This particular style incorporates free verse with the brevity of haiku. The Japanese experimented with free verse haiku, in the early part of this century.

The formal or traditional form of haiku is expressed in the writings of the poet Basho. This style has three lines with a total of seventeen syllables. There are five syllables in the first line, seven in the second, and five in the third line.

Both styles can depict the poetic nature of people, plants, animals, celestial lights, and the seasons. The haiku can express beauty, wonder, or humor with little or no need for punctuation or rhyme.

Acknowledgements

Oteka

Mary

Celest

Jessica

John

Donna

Ken

Windy

On the veranda

the cat

stretching its shadow.

Trees whispering

to the children

"come and fly your kites".

Spider leaps

from the ceiling fan

ancient bungi jumper.

1

On a reed

orange dragonfly

a flame.

Across the corner

of my imagination

shadow of a lizard.

The bird bath

quietly sunning itself

between showers.

2

Pond singing

as water falls

over night.

Nightingale's song

wrapped the evening

in splendor.

At my feet

a slice of sky

bluest little dragonfly.

3

Spring wind

grabbed my hat

with hands I could not see.

Sound of paper

over head

wind and kite conversing.

Dreaming

for a minute

in eternity.

4

Father's pipe

for many years

has been our weather vane.

Swimming

up stream   .

a salmon moon.

By the sea

sand dunes

coming and going.

5

Shedding snow

Mount Fuji

dresses for spring.

Into the night

go plums

with the stars.

Out of the night

come plums

with the dawn.

6

Lounge chair

in a shady spot

reclining.

Extra button

on my collar

sleeping ladybug.

Abandoned wheelbarrow

full of guests

bathing sparrows splashing.

7

From the edge

of my nap

crickets calling.

Breath of spring

full of fish

north of the hibachi.

Walking home

cats following

the fish market man.

8

Rainy weather
on every line
drips from eye to page.

Cock crowing
yet the doll
keeps dreaming.

Autumn alone
with the cherry trees
memories in full bloom.

9

At summer's end

the cuckoo calls

quietly for a change.

Unbearable heat

sparrows with open mouths

praying for rain.

Caught the frog

that lectured last night

outside my bedroom window.

10

Plum blossoms

fill the air

with the blush of spring.

                    Scent of jasmine

                    from the neighbor's yard

                    visits our water garden.

Broken bowl

in the rain

full of painted flowers.

11

The scarecrow

impeccably dressed

in his tattered best.

A sketch

drew my mind

to the page.

Resourceful path

at the stream

turned to stepping stones.

12

That rustling sound

from the bushes

is bigger than a lizard.

Awakened at dawn

by hundreds .

of chirping trees.

Floating birds

gently ripple

on the moonlit lake.

13

Spring births

roses and wars

what a joy, what a pity.

A candle

in the wind

red dragonfly on a reed.

Cock crowing

just before sunrise

how enlightening.

14

Occasionally

growing a tree

bonsai mountainside.

Slowly sipping

the river swallows

a bit of Hardrock Canyon.

Poppy field

fluttering in the breeze

butterflies in bloom.

15

Disguised as night

the new moon

slips by.

Butterfly

on the cold hibachi

wings ablaze.

Early morning

the mist

mooing.

16

In the middle

of nowhere

sand dunes wandering.

Wildebeest

mowing

the wilderness.

Jaws that swam

an ancient sea

withering in the desert.

17

Morning walk

on a well worn path

beside a nameless stream.

Clouds pouring

reflections

on the desert floor.

Grains of sand

building dunes

in the milky way.

18

Though snow is deep

a friend visits

with warm hands and soup.

Cdld night

the quilt

keeps shrinking.

Winter storm

painting whitecaps

on the lake.

19

Hazy evening
crossing the bridge
my head swimming.

Lost
in the forest
looking for a familiar tree.

Day and night
an ear full
of cicada songs.

20

Through plum blossoms

a light mist

guides the temple bells.

Night and plum

go their separate ways

in the dawn.

Mountain reaching

for the sky

sprouts a desert isle.

21

Butterfly

asleep on the hibachi

Sunday morning.

Winter pond

frogs are taking

their annual vacation.

Perfect day

to fly a kite

willow leaves at play.

22

Gathering flowers

among the bees

pollen on her jeans.

       Cattails

       by the river

       catching dragonflies.

Faint image

on a distant hill

flying the kite above.

23

4th of July
fireworks painting
neon palm trees.

        In the dawn
        night finds shelter
        at the far side of the sky.

Spring winds
carrying fragrant shadows
plum trees in bloom.

24

Quietly burning

at the tip of a reed

red dragonfly.

A stranger

wrapped in fog

turned out to be a neighbor.

Chattering birds

have seen the light

dawn must be moments away.

25

Tears of rust

on the hibachi

after your departure.

In the stream

painted ponies

prancing on the moon.

Colorful daydream

a cardinal on the bough

warming the winter's chill.

26

High-tech mosquitoes
buzzing, landing, biting
me.

Muddy river
panting for rain
thickens in the drought.

Quiet morning
mockingbird chasing insects
with stealth of wing and beak.

27

Sparrows gathering
at the outdoor cafe
for a bite to eat.

Evening in the garden
overhead swallows
blooming by the hundreds.

Watering flowers
swallows flying by
taking little swallows.

28

Wild frog
tamed by innocence
staring at the children.

Summer buds
tiny trees frogs
clinging to the reeds.

New moon frog
hopping through the grass
just where I can not see.

29

Autumn wind

grows winter-like teeth

devouring butterflies.

Children

chasing butterflies.

all over spring.

Bucket and sky

sharing

a vision.

30

Flowers and butterflies

came to the field

as their ancestors last spring.

Rain clouds

pouring reflections

on the desert floor.

On the mountain

streams flowing

past the winter chill.

31

Rushing river
smoothing rough edges
slowly.

The clock
joins the wind chimes
for a brief duet.

Scorching heat
drives the river
into a stream.

32

Humming

work songs

busy bees.

                    Smell of gunpowder

                    in spring grass

                    cold war thaws.

Bullets flying

through plum blossoms

wounding the heart of spring.

33

Rising river

making its way

up the path to my door.

Captured

by the roses

my heart belongs to spring.

Mountain trail

through the forest

adorned with butterflies.

34

Tucked away

in winter snow

spring rapids.

Sleeping

in the dead of winter

summer rapids

Cold wave

roaring down the mountain

in tides of an avalanche.

35

Boulder falling

from the sky

dust in the Himalayas.

This evening

a breath of sunshine

warms the autumn wind.

Early spring

tulips brilliant

in the rain.

Grandma's hands

gathering honey

among the thorns.

                    Faint call

                    of a crow

                    in the wind chimes.

The spider

rebuilding

after spring cleaning.

37

Great wind

above the bonsai

humming bird in breeze.

Sailing

through life

butterfly in breeze.

Waves of heat

tides of the sun

washing across the road.

38

Fresh bread

slice by slice

becomes the new moon.

Tomorrow

is beyond me

tonight.

Low tide

seashells beached

by the moon.

39

Windy paths

across the seas

trade winds blowing.

Strawberries ripen

far too slowly

for a youthful tongue.

Watching fireworks

smell of gunpowder

among the roses.

40

Coming and going

the only road

in town.

Winter evening

silence falling

between the snow.

Rain clouds

gave birth

to a bucket of sky.

41

Yoke of the sun
falls beyond the mountains
illuminating my dreams.

Traveling light
across the desert
dust storms.

Turning the corner
seeing his bike
just in time to sigh.

42

Dandelion children

leaving home

to join the butterfly circus.

Each spring

fragrant snow

west of the cherry trees.

The afternoon

has a whimsical smile

squirrels playing on the hammock.

43

In a field of sheep
the collie's hair
blowing like barley.

Ferrying light
across the lake
a spring moon.

Summer sun
burning bright
among the autumn leaves.

44

Departing friend

of the summer moon

autumn cuckoo.

        Thinning mist

        on distant hills

        autumn leaves ablaze.

In the dead

of winter

a moon blossoms.

45

Crumbling wall

shedding light

on the side.

Milking poinsettias

of their beauty

he places them in a vase.

Just behind

a wave of geese

the tillers.

46

The widow gazes

with tear-filled eyes

at faded photos of spring.

Children looking

out at winter

through the eyes of spring.

Asleep

on the museum bench

dreaming of landscapes.

47

Falling

through the silence

an autumn leaf.

Mosquitoes and petals

in the autumn wind

left me with mixed emotions.

Late autumn skies

full of rain

smothering crimson leaves.

48

Spring cleaning

is far behind

petals everywhere.

Dangling midair

caterpillar

at the end of the line.

Rain forest singing

way into the night

in honor of an incredible moon.

49

Exploring

the wall

roses falling over.

My neighbor's wall

is no match

for kites or curious children.

Under stars

among chattering crickets

tranquil moonbeams.

50

Flowering weeds
surviving the war
invaded my peaceful garden.

Thunder breaking
overhead
between lightning's teeth.

Busy bee
tumbles into a flower
departing all abuzz.

51

Mailbox

on a dusty road

open for suggestions.

Sun's reflection

on a cloudy day

water lilies at heart.

Spring pilgrimage

of monarch butterflies

wafting ever northward.

52

Personal opinions

singing solos

at the committee meeting.

In morning air

his after-shave dances

with her summer roses.

Ripe

the moon settles

among the melons.

53

Grandma's portrait

on the wall

touches my heart everyday.

In the neighbor's yard

white rabbit running

through full moon shadows.

Over canvas

paint brush sweeping

summer landscapes.

54

The garden

wind in leaves

autumn theater at play.

At the gate

coming and going

autumn leaves.

In the wind

a harvest moon

gathering leaves.

55

By the sea

moon sweeping

tide in, and tide out.

Gray clouds

drawing a rainy curtain

across the meadow.

At reed's tip

crimson dragonfly

burning in the wind.

56

Day and night

wave after wave

moon, sea and tide.

Snowy owl

hunting

in its reflection.

Dog barking

must be a ghost

not a soul in sight.

57

Venice skies

lavender in pink

breath of morning glories.

In the pond

a slice of the moon

wades in cherry blossoms.

From caverns

cool waters

trickle into summer.

58

Skimming skies

the dragon-flies

above the garden pond.

Thirsty rocks

sipping rainbows

by the waterfall.

Cat sitting

on the shadow of a chair

comfortably napping.

59

Apartment hunting
on the ocean floor
Mr. Hermit Crab.

By the pond
orange flowers
miming sunrise.

Sand and rock
devoured the beast
leaving a bony reflection.

60

Radiant light
looming just ahead
sunrise on the road.

       Stars brighten
       blues deepen
       sunflowers but a memory.

First snow
winter's children
at play.

61

Between two trees

a hammock smiles

under the plum blossom sky.

Fish kite flying

at the front door

celebrating a son.

Wafting

door to door

wind chimes's song.

62

On the road

a nightingale's song

shortens the journey.

From the forest

a nightingale's song

follows me home.

The weatherman

in my bones

predicting cooler days.

63

Parting trees

a highway

concealed by fog.

At the end

of my blanket

winter's breath.

Gripping all

but the candle's flame

a bitter winter's chill.

64

New Year's Day

yet the cold

seems so familiar.

Chopsticks

getting a grip

on a meal.

Skating on the lake

until dark

fireworks in celebration.

65

Sea anemone

in fresh water

fire works on the lake.

Hot petals

in the night sky

fire works on the lake.

Hailstones biting

into my roof

as if it were cotton candy.

66

Cloud of wings

above the stream

kingfisher hovering.

Winter morning

at the well

spring still buckets away.

High hopes

for an Indian summer

flew away with the geese.

67

Wild geese

pay no attention

to my little pond.

Wading deep

in the afternoon

high tide.

A familiar path

winds through the forest

all alone.

68

The waterfall

singing a duet

with a frog.

Summer wind

impatiently turning pages

while I read.

Sifting leaves

through the trees

the autumn wind.

69

Peeking out
from forest edge
a cabin along the way.

Morning mist
sipping water
at the river's edge.

Cicadas talking
into the night
winter will have the last word.

70

Heavenly tides

coming and going

clouds passing over the moon.

Stones leading

across the stream

rock of ages.

Grasshopper

upon the page

speed-reading.

71

Summer's figure

withered down

to the bones of autumn.

        Day after day

        sinking into the valley

        winter's chill.

This morning

first snowflake

of the year.

72

Saturday morning
cutting the grass
to cut the grass again.

Peach blossoms
upon the road
traveling by chance.

This evening
cicadas singing
their old favorites.

73

Yellow sun

in the shade

swallowtail butterflies.

Marina

sprouting little boats

in the bay.

The fish

jumped in

the splash.

74

Sea of green

above the waves

grassy cliffs of spring.

Misty reflection

upon the water's

muted autumn sunrise.

Looking out

over the sea

cliffs of cherry blossoms.

75

Bamboo brushes

dreaming landscapes

on a rice paper day.

Swimming in

the red snapper's eye

photographer's lens snapping.

In the wind

her veil

the autumn mist.

76

Mountains

growing bonsai trees

on the side.

Morning light

like a rooster's top

zinnias crowing.

Prehistoric flowers

wading in a vase

birds-of-paradise.

77

The gardener placed

each stepping stone

in honor of serenity.

How reassuring

each step I take

upon the stepping stones.

Stepping stones

exploring the garden

moistened by spring.

78

The garden path

encountered an old tree

and respectfully walked around it.

Little puddles

full of sky

after the spring rain.

The withered tree

has character

written all over its trunk.

79

JQuiet stream

encountering stones

babbles like a brook.

Island rooted

beneath the waves

sprouting anemone and palm.

Glowing

among the orange tulips

a spring sunrise.

80

Rainy season
clouds pouring
on the Kalahari.

Little flowers
painting landscapes
of butterflies in spring.

A hurricane
blew into town
and ruffled a few feathers.

81

An uninvited guest

crashed our garden party

that blow-hard the hurricane.

Little clouds

floating by the trellis

white clematis flowers.

Forest green hills

flowing down to shore

into an emerald sea.

Navajo blanket

woven sunset colors

warms the children's winter.

Survivors' tears

for ravaged loved ones

devoured by cancer's plague.

Paw and hoof

digging deep in summer grass

survival on the menu.

Paint peeling
in colorful layers
on the old front door.

Harvest time
on valley floor
beneath the snow-filled Alps.

Plankton simply
supporting life
what a whale of a job.

84

Riderless steed

beneath the waves

sea horse among the eelgrass.

Jungle flowers

in her hair

south sea island maiden.

Feather rainbow

warrior's raiment

ceremony in the forest

85

Cool diamonds

sparkle with fire

ancestors black as coal.

Taking off

on a paper raft

ancestors of the astronaut.

Sandy shore

sliding into the surf

setting sail with the tides.

86

Autumn's breath
slowly makes its way
down the maple mountain.

      Adobe walls
      of Santa Fe
      naturally at home.

Light falling
on an oak fence
between the afternoon shadows.

87

Strips of color

above the lake

forest green, snow white and sky blue.

During my nap

a mosquito

quietly bit me.

From now

until next year

I'll keep plum blossoms in mind.

88

Spring morning
leaves shimmering
in sun-lit breezes.

Summer heat
squeezing the river
out of the desert.

Cold day
mist streaming
from every conversation.

89

Autumn calendar

turns leaves down

and the cuckoo off.

Autumn day

silent cuckoo

leaves softly crashing.

Portrait of a cuckoo

in black and white

blown away by the autumn wind.

90

Ocean waves

leaping at the moon

touching the hem of the shore.

At the grave site

falling cherry blossoms

burying one another.

Waterfall

at the pond

sings a moving song.

91

Fireflies dancing

just off shore

house boats in the bay.

On the horizon

dark storm clouds

marching toward my wind chimes.

Eager to travel

the melting snow

slips away to the sea.

92

Late spring

bee after bee

flying by the cherry tree.

Waving goodbye

closer than ever

a distant cousin.

Glowing

in the rivers face

a summer afternoon.

93

Dragons

waiting

by the river.

      Water birds

      feathered rainbows

      descending from the sky.

Rainbow fish

among the coral

bathed in eternal rain.

Locked in winter

released by spring

plum blossoms bursting.

Silhouette at sunset

forest in light

of a cuckoo's cry.

Brilliant dream

in morning light

falling cherry blossoms.

95

Moon above

the moon on the lake

circling the night.

Summer evening

breeze painting

a fragrant collage.

The mountain path

opens and closes

in the forest mist.

Summer wind
arranging butterflies
in the meadow.

Prehistoric jaws
at the watering hole
come alive in a flash.

Suddenly
river rock
brandishing teeth.

97

Snake catcher
digging cautiously
for his treasure.

The monsoon
wringing wet
came ashore.

In the drizzle
a bell softly rings
this autumn morning.

98

Evening sun

on the windowsill

a tomato ripens.

Heron fishing

at river's edge

catching comets.

From the ledge

boulders become pebbles

and the river a stream.

99

Bell's last toll

flies away with the geese

over the horizon.

Calling the leaves

to come and rest

a graying autumn wind.

The moon and I

stayed up all night

staring at one another.

100